Indoor Gardening

The Ultimate Beginner's Guide to Growing an Indoor Garden

Emerson Woods

© 2015

Table of Contents

Introduction

Chapter 1: Let the Journey Begin

Chapter 2: Location

Chapter 3: Lighting

Chapter 4: Containers

Chapter 5: Planting Medium

Chapter 6: Planting

Chapter 7: Pollination

Chapter 8: Watering

Chapter 9: Fertilizing

Chapter 10: Temperature and Humidity Control

Chapter 11: Pest Control

Chapter 12: Final General Thoughts

Appendix

Carrots

Tomatoes

Peppers

Eggplants

Radishes

Potatoes

Conclusion

Bonus Book 1: Backpacking

Bonus Book 2: Camping Tips

Thank You

Free Gift

Emerson Woods Copyright © 2015

All rights reserved. No part of this book may be reproduced in any form without permission in writing from the author. Reviewers may quote brief passages in reviews.

Disclaimer

No part of this publication may be reproduced or transmitted in any form or by any means, mechanical or electronic, including photocopying or recording, or by any information storage and retrieval system, or transmitted by email without permission in writing from the publisher.

While all attempts and efforts have been made to verify the information held within this publication, neither the author nor the publisher assumes any responsibility for errors, omissions, or opposing interpretations of the content herein.

This book is for entertainment purposes only. The views expressed are those of the author alone, and should not be taken as expert instruction or commands. The reader of this book is responsible for his or her own actions when it comes to reading the book.

Adherence to all applicable laws and regulations, including international, federal, state, and local governing professional licensing, business practices, advertising, and all other aspects of doing business in the US, Canada, or any other jurisdiction is the sole responsibility of the purchaser or reader.

Neither the author nor the publisher assumes any responsibility or liability whatsoever on the behalf of the purchaser or reader of these materials.

Any received slight of any individual or organization is purely unintentional.

Introduction

First and foremost I want to thank you for downloading the book, "Indoor Gardening The Ultimate Guide Beginner's Guide to Growing an Indoor Garden".

In this book you will learn how to grow a beautiful indoor garden that will not only produce great tasting food for your family, but also compliment the looks of your home. You will learn all types of secrets within the confines of this book, including how to choose the correct location for your indoor garden, advantages and disadvantages of the many types of indoor lighting, and what containers work best for indoor gardening. Additionally, you will learn the best practices for planting your garden, how to pollinate indoor plants, and the basics of water and fertilizing the garden. Where possible, this book provides solutions using supplies that you may already have on hand. No garden is without problems. Therefore, we cover the best solutions in temperature control, watering, fertilizing, and pest control. If you have never gardened before, then this book is for you. Likewise, if you have gardened inside for years, you will learn tricks and tips that will allow you to grow a more bountiful crop.

After the basic instructions, applicable to most plants, we have included specific instructions for many popular indoor plants. These plants include carrots, tomatoes, peppers, eggplants, radishes and potatoes. In this section, you will learn specific tips and tricks to enlarge your indoor garden harvest.

Thanks again for downloading this book, I hope you enjoy it!

Chapter 1 Let the Journey Begin

Close your eyes for a minute and picture yourself taking a big bite from a tasty tomato that you have grown. Feel the juice as it drains down your throat. Imagine the things that you can make from garden fresh tomatoes.

Alternatively, picture yourself biting into a crisp carrot from your garden. Is there anything that tastes better? Again, imagine the things that you can do with garden-fresh carrots.

Now, open your eyes and look outside. Is there a foot of snow on the ground? Alternatively, it may be 100 degrees outside with no sign of relief in sight.

Neither extreme heat nor snow seems conducive to growing garden fresh vegetables. There is an easy solution that allows you to grow wonderful food regardless of what the weather decides to do. That answer is indoor gardening.

Indoor gardening lets you feed your family garden fresh vegetables year round. You are not reliant on receiving the right amount of rain. You control the temperatures so your crops neither freeze nor burn up. The great news is that it is easy to garden inside.

There is no doubt about it; produce from gardens tastes better than produce from the grocery store. One of the reasons is that commercial growers do not particularly care how their produce tastes. Instead, they care about growing produce that will withstand rough treatment. They also care about growing produce that travels well so that they can ship it around the world. Finally, they are concerned about the cost to produce each item.

There are two types of indoor gardening, hydroponics and container. While hydroponics allows you to grow a large amount of plants in a very small area, this book will focus on the more traditional container gardening. That way, you can decide the size of the garden that is right for you. It also allows you to keep your budget firmly in mind.

Chapter 2 Location

The first step in planting your indoor garden is to determine the correct location in your home for the garden. Plants require three things to grow. They need air, water, and light. Considering each one of these requirements will help you choose the right location.

When considering a location for your indoor garden, you need to decide which type of vegetable you are most likely to grow so that you can choose an area of your home that is the right temperature.

Cool season vegetables including turnips, broccoli, spinach, cabbage, kohlrabi, onions, lettuce, radishes and peas do best when the temperature is about 40 degrees. Semi-hardy plants including most herbs, beets, potatoes, carrots and cauliflower do best in temperatures ranging from 40 degrees to 50 degrees. Warm season crops including summer squash, beans, celery, cucumbers, and tomatoes do best where the temperature stays above 60 degrees and can tolerate temperatures up to 95 degrees.

Plants need air to grow. That air should be draft free. Therefore, when choosing an area within your home, make sure to choose one that is free from drafts caused by outdoor doors. This is especially important if you will be garden when it is extremely cold outside, as one cold blast can kill all your hard work.

Additionally, choose an area that is not near any vents in your home. These vents blow hot air in the winter and cool air in the summer. This can stress out the plants and they will not produce properly. Additionally, the air blowing on the plants can cause them to dry out quickly putting them under even more stress.

Generally, you will want to avoid the garage. This area often experiences extreme heat variations as it often becomes too hot in the summer and too cold in the winter.

Unless you have a finished attic, then it can be hard to grow plants in this area. The summer heat in many attics makes it hard for many plants to grow.

The second thing that plants need to grow is water. When considering the water needs of your garden, think about how you will get the water to each plant. If you have a small garden, then a watering can is probably a good answer. As the size of your garden grows, you may need to locate it near a water source so that you have easy access or can hook up a misting system.

Additionally, it is likely that you will get some water on the floor when you are gardening. You may spill some while you are watering the plants, or some may run out of the plant containers. Additionally, the leaves may release water from time to time. Think about how you plan to control water so that it does not damage the floor. You may want to garden in an area that has a tile floor so that it is easy to mop up any spills.

Indoor gardeners also need to consider controlling the humidity in the growing area. This is particularly a problem when the outdoor climate is dry. Therefore, the garden should be placed where the plants can be misted on a regular basis. Additionally, create a space where you can place a large tray containing lava rocks and water near the plants. Consider running a humidifier in the house if you already do not have one.

Chapter 3 Lighting

The third component that all plants must have is light. Chances are that even if you grow your plants by a window that gets light throughout the day, your plants will not get enough light. Therefore, it is crucial to think about how you will supply additional light.

Lighting is very crucial because plants need light to photosynthesize. A plant requires photosynthesis to turn water and carbon dioxide into the food that it needs to thrive. The plant's photoreceptors require the same wavelength of light as the sun to enable this process to occur.

Some plants that you may choose to grow are long-day plants that require up to 16 hours of light each day. Common examples of long-day plants include most herbs, beets, cucumbers, lettuce, radishes, and turnips. If these plants do not get enough light, they will be lighter in color than normal, have thin stems and very small leaves. They will not thrive and will not produce the crop that you are hoping to receive.

Other plants are short-day plants that require light up to 12 hours a day. Some common examples include potatoes, okra and cucumbers. If short day plants are exposed to too many hours of sunlight they will not bloom.

Alternatively, some plants like tomatoes and onions depends on the variety chosen so you will need to check on the seed package to see how many hours are needed.

Most indoor gardeners discover that they need additional lighting in order to be successful. Gardeners have many different choices. In most cases, however, incandescent lights should not be used because they do not give off enough light and it is the wrong spectrum.

One choice is to use florescent lighting. These lights are best when used with cool-season short-day crops, as they do not require a lot of light. They should be avoided all together when plants are budding and flowering, as they do not give off enough light.

Another choice that gardeners may want to consider is compact florescent lights. These lights are ideal for most plants as they produce enough light for most plants to thrive. These lights are cooler than more traditional florescent lights. Therefore, they can be placed closer to the plant to provide more light without burning the plant.

High pressure sodium bulbs produce light in the red-orange spectrum which can really benefit plants when they are flowering. Alternatively, these lights do not produce light in the blue-spectrum that is needed for a leaf growth. Therefore, they should be coupled with another light source so that you get the maximum crop production.

Metal halide (MH) bulbs produce blue-white light that encourages leaf growth. Therefore, many gardeners combine them with high pressure sodium lights to produce a complete lighting system. These bulbs can be expensive, however, each bulb lasts about 10,000 hours.

The next question that a gardener must address is how many watts are right for their garden. Generally, a 400 watt bulb will cover an eight foot square area where the plants can get some sun through a window. When no sun is present, then the bulb can cover a five foot square area. A 600 watt bulb can cover a ten foot square area when the plants can get some sun through a window. The same bulb can cover a seven foot square area when the plant can get no sun. Finally, a 1000 watt bulb can cover a 12 foot square area when the plant can get some sun through a window, and an eight foot square area when it cannot.

The gardener must also consider how close to the plant that the light needs to be to maximize its use. Generally, a 400 wat bulb needs to be no more than four feet above the plants. A 600 watt bulb should be between 1.5 feet and 5 feet above the plants, while a 1000 watt bulb should be between 2 feet and 6 feet above the plants.

When thinking about the lighting system, gardeners need to consider where the light will plug in. This is especially true if more than one light is needed for the garden. You will be moving in the area often so you will not want countless extension cords present as they can present a trip and fall hazard.

Chapter 4 Containers

A variety of containers can be used as pots for plants depending on what you decide to grow and how fancy you want the plants to look. When choosing the right container for your plants, you need to consider what the container is made of, what size pot is right for your plant, and what you need to put under your plant to catch excess water.

Containers can be almost anything from recyclable plastic grocery bags to expensive concrete pots. One of the most popular options are terracotta pots. These pots are often modestly expensive. Some are made for more decorative purposes than others. Therefore, you need to make sure that you have great drainage holes in the bottom. If you do not drop and break them, they can be used multiple times, although if you do not clean them properly, they can be a breeding ground for bacteria. Some plant's root systems dry out faster in terracotta pots than in other options. Therefore, the gardener must water more consistently. Alternatively, if you tend to overwater, these pots may be the perfect solution, because their porous surface makes it almost impossible to overwater. If you do not give the pots enough light, they can develop a green moss on their sides.

Glazed ceramic pots are a great addition to an indoor garden. There are a variety of designs available so you can choose one that suits your personal style. If you are unsure if your indoor garden will get too hot, then this pot may be the perfect choice, because the pot insulates the root system. Many of these pots do not have a good drainage system. If that is the case with a glazed ceramic pot that you like, then make sure to fill the bottom with about two inches of gravel to aid in drainage.

Concrete pots can be some of the most expensive pots to buy. If you are considering a large concrete pot, then it can be extremely heavy making it difficult to move. Additionally, the weight often means that this pot should be placed directly on the floor on top of a floor joint. If you are considering growing trees inside, then concrete pots are your best choice because they are strong enough to control the root system.

There are many advantages to plastic pots. There lightweight design makes them the perfect choice for moving from one location to another during the growing season. While plastic pots used to be ugly, gardeners find a wide variety of colorful choices today making them a great choice when incorporating a garden into a room. Plastic pots maximize the plants ability to use every drop of water that it receives. These pots can be used many times. Additionally, many are made of recycled materials and can be recycled when they are no longer useful. Yet, another advantage of these pots is that they heat and cool quickly so that plants are better able to maintain the temperature that they need to thrive. Some are very thin. Therefore, they can break easily, especially when plants with strong root structures are placed in them.

Authentic stone pots can be very heavy, but they can have a lot of character. Many stone pots today are made from faux stone. Gardeners will generally find a wider variety of choices in faux stone pots. In addition, these pots are generally lighter in weight, but many do not have the charm of real stone pots. Most stone pots last for years and are extremely durable. Most are good insulators of heat making them a great choice for plants that need a higher temperature to thrive.

Wooden pots are available in a variety of styles. Many, however, have been treated with a sealant that is not safe to use when growing food. They should generally be avoided for growing food. This is especially true of the older ones.

Chapter 5 Planting Medium

The gardener must decide which planting medium is right for their indoor gardeners. The truth of the matter is that the best is usually a combination of several, but examining them one at a time allows you to understand why you would want to use them.

There was a time not long ago that everything was planted in peat moss. That is not the case today, because the gathering of peat moss destroys insect habitats in bogs. In addition, scientists have discovered that using peat moss often leads to the spread of disease within a garden. When peat moss is combined with other types of soil, it compacts the soil and reduces the air that gets to the plant's roots.

Therefore, the only plants that should be planted in peat moss are acid-loving plants that seem to love this soil. Peat moss has a pH balance of about 4. This allows acid loving plants to get iron from the soil that they cannot otherwise obtain.

Unlike peat moss, sphagnum moss floats on top of the water. Its collection is not considered to be an environmental danger. When planting seeds, a little bit of sphagnum moss is helpful in fighting the fungal disease commonly called damping off which kills many young plants. Do not use too much sphagnum moss, however, because it can take water away from your plant's root system. The use of sphagnum moss encourages better airflow around the root system when mixed with other soils.

Bark is a byproduct of the timber industry. When mixed with other types of soil, bark encourages excellent drainage. It also is less expensive than peat or sphagnum moss. Bark tends to encourage plants to dry out faster when compared against other mediums.

Perlite is white volcanic rock that is crushed. Most perlite comes from Turkey and is sterile. Gardeners find different grades of perlite and the best one to use will be marked as coarse, as the fine and medium grades tend to work their way to the top of the plant's surface and wash away. The sterile nature of perlite ensures that you are not introducing new diseases to your container plants through its use. When perlite is mixed with soil, plants benefit from additional aeration. Additionally, perlite can hold up to four times its weight in water helping to ensure that the soil stays moist. It does, however, lose the water weight quickly, so plants can dry out faster than with other options.

Vermiculite is a popular choice with many container gardeners. It should never be used by itself as it can expand and hold up to 300 percent of its weight in water. Therefore, it can cause plants to dry out very quickly. It does, however, greatly improve drainage in container gardens. Likewise, its use helps to ensure that the plant gets the proper aeration.

Coconut fiber is quickly becoming a popular growing medium around the world, because it is a completely renewable resource. Gardeners should avoid coconut fiber that is high in sea salt, because it is too fine in texture to work properly. Coconut fiber retains more oxygen allowing plants to grow properly. In addition, it has excellent water holding abilities. Finally, coconut fiber stimulates root hormones helping plants to grow stronger.

Sterilized soil is a great alternative for many plants, especially when mixed with a substance that will help it retain water better. The process used to sterilize the soil ensures that no weeds are present. This soil is rich in nitrogen, magnesium, and potassium, all which encourage plants to grow healthy. Its fine texture allows roots to grow easily.

The best soil for your indoor garden is usually a combination of many of these mediums. The experts at Michigan State University Extension suggests that you use one-third part sphagnum peat moss or coconut fiber, one-third part vermiculite, and one-third part screened compost to make your own potting soil at home.

Later, consider switching to a combination of sterile soil, compost and sand or small gravel. The gravel helps the plant get proper drainage, while the compost feeds the plant. The sterile soil helps feed the plant, as well as providing strength to the roots.

You can make sterile soil at home, although it will smell awful while you are making it. Preheat the oven to 200 degrees. Put a small amount of soil on a baking tray. Bake the soil until it reaches a temperature of 180 degrees, and then bake it for another 30 minutes. Allow the soil to cool completely before using it.

Gardeners have many choices when it comes to the planting medium that they choose. For starting plants, the best is usually a combination of sphagnum moss or coconut fiber, combined with vermiculite and compost. When your plants mature enough to be transplanted, then it is time to switch to sterile soil, compost and sand or gravel.

Chapter 6 Planting

You have now made many important decisions about your indoor garden. You have decided on the right location for your garden, secured the proper lighting, and brought or recycled your containers. You have also decided what planting medium best meets your needs. Now is the time to start growing your plants.

Some crops including garlic, onions, carrots, beets, radishes, spinach and greens love the cold weather. These seeds should be placed in a bag of moist sand and put in the refrigerator for at least one month prior to planting.

All cool season crops and most warm season crops that have larger seeds including corn, squash and eggplants benefit from soaking before they are planted. Some fruit seeds including melons also do better if you soak the seed.

If you determine that your seed needs soaked, then fill up a bowl of water with hot tap water. Place seeds in the water and allow them to sit for 18 hours. You are now ready to plant these seeds.

Many large seeds also benefit from scarification. This process is also simple. Just rub the seed for 20 seconds across a piece of rough sandpaper. Then, soak the seed and plant as usual.

Even if you have purchased new pots, it is a great idea to sterilize them before you plant in them. The process is simple, and can eliminate many plant diseases in the days ahead. Start by mixing a ten percent solution of bleach and water. Then, soak the pots in the solution for 30 minutes. Allow the pots to dry before continuing.

Now, place a large tray that has sides that are at least two inches deep on a flat surface. Pour boiling water into the tray until the water is one inch deep. Then, place your pots on the tray and let them sit for at least 30 minutes. This ensures that the soil is moist when you begin to plant your seeds.

The next step is to remove the pot from the tray and label it with what you plan to plant in it as well as the date. Read the seed packet to see how deep you should plant the seed as it may vary based on the type of plant you are growing. Plant three seeds per pot for each pot that you want to survive. This will allow you to thin your plants later allowing the best ones to survive. Once you have planted the seed, return the pot to the pan of water. Continue until you have planted all of your pots.

You now should prepare the place that you want the plants to germinate. Start by laying a piece of Styrofoam on a flat surface. While you can use larger pieces, Styrofoam plates will work.

Now, cover the Styrofoam with your heating mat. These mats are waterproof. The size of the mat that you need depends on the number of plants that you want to germinate at one time. Look for a heating mat that has a long enough cord to easily reach your electrical plug-in. When purchasing a mat, look for one that has a thermometer that allows you to test the soil temperature easily. Finally, look for a heating mat that has multiple temperature zones if you plan on germinating several types of plants at the same time.

If you do not have a heating mat, and do not choose to buy one at this time, then you can sit the plants on top of the refrigerator. The heat given off by the refrigerator will be enough to help them germinate.

Wherever you choose to put the plants, you should cover them loosely with plastic wrap. This helps to keep the moisture in place. Then, it is a waiting game until your plants germinate. The length of time that you must wait depends on the plant.

The first thing that you will see come through the ground will be the cotyledons. While these will look similar to leaves, the cotyledon works to feed the plant until the first leaves appear in a few days.

Once the leaves appear, then place your plants under the growing lights keeping them as close to the plants as you can. Supply your plants with at least 14 hours of light each day. As your plants grow, you will need to move the growing lights to adjust for their height. It is best to transplant the plants to their permanent homes when they have at least two leaves.

You may encounter some problems shortly after your plants germinate. The most common is drying out. Thankfully, it is easily solved by simply placing the pot back in a tray of water for 30 minutes. If this occurs, make sure that your soil tests for the right temperature and that you have the plastic wrap in place.

Another problem that you may encounter is algae. Therefore you should check the soil's surface on a regular basis for the sign of any green or black substance. If you discover algae, then you should immediately transplant the young plant. Transplanting at this stage can be difficult because the root structure can break very easily. Therefore, make sure to work very carefully.

A third problem that occurs occasionally is damping off. One of the earliest signs of damping off is that the plant's color will be lighter than it should be for its variety. You may also notice that the stem seems extremely small. The main cause for this is that the lights are not close enough to the pots. If the problem continues, then use a fungicide to treat the plant.

As your plants grow, you will need to transplant them to their permanent homes. Start by working over paper or other surface that you can easily clean up as a small amount of potting media will escape through this hole.

Grab the plant by its stem and turn the pot upside down. This allows you to gently coax the plant from its current home to move it to its new home. Then, fill around the plant with potting soil leaving about one inch at the top of the plant. In most cases, you should transplant one plant per pot.

You are now well on the way to growing your vegetables and fruit inside. You have successfully planted your seeds, germinated them, and transplanted them to their new pots. While you have worked hard, you will soon enjoy your rewards.

Chapter 7 Pollination

The easiest crops to grow in an indoor garden are those that self-pollinate like most greens, lettuce, beans, peas, celery, some tomatoes, and some peppers, self-pollinate so you do not have to worry about pollinating these plants. For other plants that you want to grow in your indoor garden, you will need to help the pollination process along. If you are unsure, you can use this technique on all your plants without suffering any negative consequences.

It is important to know which plants are males and which plants are female. In most cases, male plants will put on their flowers first. This is a good time to label the plants that have put on the first flowers if you are raising a large number of plants.

A few days later, the female plant will put on its first flowers. Confirm that it is a female plant, by looking for a very small swelling just below the flower. Additionally, if you look directly into the flower where the stigma is located, you should see an irregularly shaped lobed ball.

Now, examine the male plant and look directly into the center of the flower. You should see a central stigma surrounded by anthers.

Take a cotton swab and rough up the end of it a little. Do not tear the cotton off the swab stick. Then, carefully insert the cotton swab into the male flower ensuring that you come in contact with the male anthers. Turn the cotton swab gently to gather the pollen. You may or may not be able to see the pollen.

Now, go to the female plant and rub the same end of the cotton swab against the stigma on the inside of the flower. Return to the male flower and again swab the end. You have now successfully pollinated the first flower. Continue until you have pollinated all of the flowers.

If you do not have the success that you want in pollinating the flowers, then wait a few days until the plant puts on new flowers. Then, try again.

There are several reasons that pollination may not be successful. The first of these is that your plants are not getting enough light. Examine the plant to see if the leaves are cupping upward. If the plant is near a window, look at the direction that the plant is growing. If it is growing toward the light, then it is probably searching for new light. Examine the most recent growth and see if it looks different from previous growth. If it does, then you need to adjust your growing lights to be closer to the plant. You may also need to leave the lights on longer.

The second reason that your pollination may not be successful is that your plant has not gotten enough moisture. In general, the soil will be darker and you will notice that the dirt on top looks dry and may be pulling away from the sides of the pot.

The third reason that pollination may not be successful is that the plant lacks the nutrients that it needs to thrive. When this is the case, you need to change your fertilizing routine to increase the available nutrients.

Plants outside pollinate in many different ways. If the plant you are attempting to grow is a self-pollinator, then it will pollinate in the same way indoors. If not, then you will need to help the plant by transferring the pollen from a male plant to a female plant using a cotton swab.

Chapter 8 Watering

Improper watering may often cause major problems for the indoor gardener. Too much water and the plant often gets sick. Too little water and the plant does not produce a bountiful crop. Therefore, it is essential to learn to water your plants properly.

Different plants have different watering requirements. Therefore, it is essential that you know the watering requirements of your individual plant. It is essential to stick your finger in the dirt about one inch to determine if the plant needs water. Plants that are droopy and shrunken may be that way because you have been overwatering or they may be that way because you need to water.

Some vegetables that like wet soil include peppers, tomatoes, and cucumbers. Some vegetables that like dry conditions include okra, squash, corn, carrots and zucchini. A great place to find out how much water your plant needs is on the seed packet.

When you have determined that it is time to water your plants, then lift the pot. Pay special attention to how the pot feels. Now, water the plant's roots, but not its leaves. Pouring water over the leaves, sets up conditions that often lead to plants getting diseased.

After you have watered the plant, then feel the weight of the pot again. After a while, you will become skilled at picking up the pot and knowing by its weight rather it needs watered or not.

Do not rely on watering meters to tell you when your plant needs watered. These meters think that all plants need the same amount of water, and that is simply not the truth.

Watering is one of the basics that you must conquer to be a successful indoor gardener. Learn how your pots feel when they need water. Never water the leaves, but concentrate on providing water to the roots.

Chapter 9 Fertilizing

One thing that you will need to do to get the best harvest is to fertilize on a regular basis. While you may have chosen to add compost to your soil when you initially replanted your plant, until the plant has numerous flowers, you will need a fertilizer that is high in nitrogen. Nitrogen helps the plant's stem grow strong, as well as helping the plant's leaves to develop. The easiest type of nitrogen fertilizer to use is a spray on short-term fertilizer.

While you can find fertilizers high in nitrogen in many different places, you can easily make one at home. The advantage of making it at home is that it saves you lots of money.

In order to make this fertilizer, simply combine three gallons of grass clippings and 1.5 gallons of water in a five gallon bucket. Use a stick or other object to stir well. You will need to let this mixture sit for three days stirring each day. At the end of three days, stir the mixture one more time and then put as much as you would like in a spray bottle. Spray the plants liberally ensuring that you soak the surface very well. Skip the next day and then repeat again.

In this way, you are sure to give the plant all the nitrogen that it needs. After five days, it is best to discard any mixture that is left. Then, you can skip a week. If the plant is not in full bloom, then make another batch and spray it again.

After the plant is in full bloom, then you will need to switch to a fertilizer that is high in potassium. Potassium is essential at this point, because it keeps the plant's roots healthy.

An easy low-cost alternative to buying potassium fertilizers in the store is to combine one tablespoon of Epsom salt in a gallon of water. Stir until it is well dissolved. Then, drench your plants with it. You can use this throughout the growing season until your plants are done bearing fruit.

All plants need to be fertilized regularly throughout the growing season. Start by fertilizing with a nitrogen based fertilizer until the flowers are in place. Then, switch to a potassium based fertilizer for the remainder of the growing season. Doing these simple steps will help ensure that you have a bountiful harvest.

Chapter 10 Temperature and Humidity Control

One of the main problems that many indoor gardeners face is temperature control. Most plants grow well between 70 and 75 degrees. Temperatures above 85 degrees can quickly damage even the hardiest of warm weather crops. Therefore, you will need to control the temperature where your plants are growing very carefully.

The first step in doing this is to obtain a good quality indoor thermometer. Position it directly under your grow lights and take a reading several times a day. If you have the plants positioned near a window, you may discover that the temperature rises dramatically throughout the day. Additionally, make sure to consider what the temperature may get too if you turn off the air conditioning while you are away during the day.

If you discover that your plants are getting too warm, there are several things that you can do. The first is to increase air circulation around the plants. You can do this simply by using fans and keeping them blowing on your plants throughout the day, but especially when light is coming in a nearby window.

If you choose this option, however, make sure to check the moisture in the soil on a regular basis. Air movement will usually dry out soil faster than when there is no movement. Therefore, you may find that you need to water more often.

Another alternative that you may want to consider is installing vents in the growing area. Just like bathroom vents, these vents will whisk away the hottest air. The new air will be much cooler than the air that was whisked away. In most areas of the country, you will need to contract with a professional electrician to get this job done.

You can also choose to install portable evaporative coolers near the plants. These units can considerably lower a room temperature in an area and operate on a regular 120-volt plug. There are several different styles including portable coolers, mobile coolers, down discharge coolers, window units and side discharge units. In fact, you may find that your plants thrive under evaporative air because it also adds moisture to the air. This option works best in areas where there is little humidity.

Yet, another option that you may want to consider is installing a ductless air conditioning system in the room. Again, this will probably require professional installation.

While you are thinking about how to keep the area cool enough, you may also want to consider how to increase the humidity in the growing area. Common symptoms of the plants not having enough humidity in the environment include leaves turning brown on tips, leaf edges turning yellow, and the flowers and leaves shriveling up or falling off quickly.

There are some simple solutions that you may want to try. The first is to mist the plants on a regular basis with tepid water.

A second low-cost method that you may want to try is grouping plants together. When plants are grouped, they trap air and moisture between them similar to a trees in a forest.

You can also set a tray of water filled with lava rocks near the plants. As the water evaporates, it will raise the humidity around the plants.

Finally, you can use a humidifier to add moisture to the area. If you choose this option, then why not get one big enough for your room if you share it with the plants. Your skin and the skin of your family members will thank you.

Chapter 11 Pest Control

Pests are usually not as big a problem for indoor gardeners as they are for outdoor gardeners. Nonetheless, there are several pests that you may encounter.

The best way to make sure that you do not encounter these pests is to practice good prevention. Prevention is a three step process. First, clear away any debris and plant matter. Secondly, inspect plants on a daily basis making sure to inspect the underside of leaves regularly. Third, if you have any suspicion that a plant might have problems, isolate that plant immediately.

Despite your best efforts, you may discover that you may encounter some common pest problems. One of those problems may be aphids. They can be hard to spot because they generally live on the underside of leaves and are less than 1/8 inch long. Making them even harder to identify, these insects come many different colors including orange, green, and black. The easiest way to identify an aphid problem is to look for a honeydew-like substance on the leaves.

If you have an aphid problem, then isolate the plant immediately. An adult female does not have to have a male partner in order to lie eggs. They often lay six to eight eggs during a day, so the problem can spread extremely quickly.

Once you have isolated the plant, then inspect each leaf for aphids. If you find some leaves are heavily invested, remove those leaves from the plant.

The next step is to use an insecticidal soap. You can make this soap at home by combining one-half tablespoon of Castile or Murphy's Oil Soap in a quart of water. Both products should be readily available in most large box stores. Then, put the mixture in a spray bottle. Spray the plant thoroughly paying special attention to the underside of the leaves.

The next step is to use a horticultural oil. You can easily make this oil at home by simply combining one tablespoon of dish soap with one cup of oil. Put the mixture in a jar and label it plainly. Now, measure out three tablespoons of the oil and combine it with two cups of tepid water. Put it in a spray bottle and shake until it combines well. Then, spray the plant completely, again paying special attention to the underside of the leaves.

While you should not have to repeat the treatment, you should not place the plant near other plants until you are sure that you have killed all the aphids.

Another problem that can occur are earwigs. These insects have flattened elongated bodies and are about 3/4 inch long. They are normally dark brown or black in color. They love to eat on tender plant shoots, so it may be one of the earliest problems that you encounter. Additionally, watch for small holes in the foliage.

There are over 20 different species of earwigs in the United States alone. They often live around the bottom of plants, so make sure to check the bottom of the pots and any saucers that you are using on a regular basis.

If you discover earwigs, then the easiest way to get rid of them is to trap them. Make some small holes in the bottom of an empty tuna fish can. Then, sprinkle some oatmeal in the can. Set the can under the plant and leave it overnight. In the morning time, you will want to check for earwigs. If you trapped any, then kill them by dunking them in a bucket of soapy water.

Unfortunately, earwigs can spread throughout your home. Therefore, it is essential that you check along the edges of your carpet for earwigs. They can be trapped here too.

Another common problem on many indoor garden plants is fungus gnats. These gnats start their life cycle as wormlike larvae with a translucent body and a black head. As they mature, they look like mosquitos, being about 1/8 inch long. They have dark wings and look like an upside down Y when looking at them from the front.

The easiest way to get rid of fungus gnats is to be sure that you let the top one to two inches of soil dry out before you water the plant again. You can also set a small bowl of vinegar mixed with dish soap near the plants. They are attracted to the smell of the vinegar, while the dish soap keeps them trapped.

A fourth common problem with indoor gardens is mealybugs. Adults are about 1/4 inch long and are usually white or gray in color. While they are usually harmless in small numbers, in larger numbers they turn leaves yellow.

Female mealybugs lay a sack on the underside of leaves that look like a small white cotton sack. If you notice these, it is essential to pull them off the leaf. These sacks contain up to

600 mealybug larvae that will emerge as a fluffy looking white or gray worm. There are up to 275 different species of mealybugs in the United States alone.

The easiest way to control mealybugs is to either prune the cotton-like sacks off the plants. If you cannot pull them off, then dip a cotton swab in some rubbing alcohol and rub the alcohol on the sack.

If you find a plant with adult mealybugs, then you can use a soft towel dipped in rubbing alcohol to wipe the leaves. Wait about three days, and then wash the rubbing alcohol off with water.

Generally, pests are less of a problem for indoor gardeners than outdoor gardeners. Some pests, however, may be present. Therefore, it is important to isolate plants that may be infected so that the infestation does not spread. In particular, aphids, earwigs, fungus gnats, and mealybugs can be a problem. Easy home treatments using readily available supplies can be used to treat these problems.

Chapter 12 Final General Thoughts

You now know how to grow a successful indoor garden. Start by choosing the right location in your home. Usually a south facing window is best because it usually gets the most light during the day. All plants need a minimum of ten hours of light during the day and many need much more.

Since most plants do not get enough light through available windows, it is usually necessary to add additional lighting to the indoor gardening area. There are numerous options available, so consider your choice carefully.

Before you can start gardening, it is vital to choose the right containers. While you can choose from a variety of construction material, it is important that all have great drainage holes in the bottom.

You will need to choose the right planting medium. Again, you have many different choices. You will need two different planting mediums, although they will share some common characteristics. In most cases, the germination planting medium needs to be a combination of equal parts of sphagnum moss or coconut fiber, vermiculite and compost. After the first true leaves appear and you are transplanting your plants, then switch to an equal mixture of sterile soil, compost, and sand or gravel.

After you make these important decisions, then you will be ready for planting. You may need to soak many seeds for a few hours before you plant them to encourage germination. Larger seeds may need scarification to germinate as the outside shell may be too strong otherwise. It is vital to plant the seeds at the right depth, so do your research before planting.

As your plant begins to put on its flowers, you may need to pollinate the plants. While this occurs naturally in nature, your environment may require that you help the process along with a cotton swab on plants that are not self-pollinating.

It is vital to water your plants with the right amount of water. Concentrate on watering the plant's roots. Avoid watering the leaves, as this can set up conditions for diseases to invade your crops.

Like watering, it is vital that you control the plant's temperature as it can vary widely throughout the day. You may need to add additional ventilation to the area so that you can keep temperatures under control. Likewise, plants need the right amount of humidity.

Finally, it is vital to control for pests by isolating any diseased plants immediately. Learn to recognize common insects that may attack your plants. Then, know how to treat that infestation using methods that do not harm your plants nor people coming in contact with them.

Before you can truly be successful at indoor gardening, you must consider the needs of the individual plant. That is the purpose of the appendix in this book.

Appendix

The purpose of this appendix is to provide specific information on plants that thrive in indoor environments. The information contained on these pages will help you know just the right methods so that you can raise a bountiful crop. When choosing heirloom varieties look for those from open seed. That way you can save the seeds and grow the same crop again.

Carrots

Carrots are a popular crop for indoor gardeners. They are easy to grow and so make an outstanding first crop. The easiest carrots to grow indoors are short carrots as they do not require a large container.

Heirloom Varieties: There are many wonderful varieties of heirloom carrots that are perfect for the indoor garden. These include Danver's 126 Half Long, Little Finger Carrots, Parisienne Carrots

Varieties: There are also other varieties that you may want to consider that are not open-pollinated. They include Thumbelina, Short 'N Sweet, Chatenny

Containers: The container for growing carrots should be at least two inches longer than the expected height of the carrot.

Planting: Carrot seeds are extremely small. Therefore, you will not be able to position the carrot seeds when planting. Instead, just toss them on top of your prepared pot. When the plants are about two-inches tall, then thin them, so that they are about two inches apart.

Temperature and Light Requirements: Carrots love about 15 hours of light each day. They are a cool-weather crop, so carefully maintain temperatures at about 65 degrees.

Watering Requirements: Carrots like moist soil, so be sure to water on a regular basis.

Harvesting: Most varieties of carrots mature between 55 and 70 days depending on the individual variety chosen. Carrots can be harvested for several weeks with each crop getting progressively longer.

Seed Saving: Carrots are biennial. Therefore, you will only get a crop in the second year. In order to save the seeds, allow the seed heads to fully ripen on the plant. Cut the entire head off and place it in a container that is not airtight. Once you are sure that the head is completely dry, shake the bag and collect the seeds.

Tomatoes

Imagine the joy of eating a fresh tomato in the middle of winter. Indoor gardeners find a great variety of tomatoes that can be grown successfully indoors. You will be amazed at the beautiful taste of these tomatoes that you have grown.

Heirloom Varieties: Gardeners have many choices when it comes to heirloom tomatoes. When looking for small tomatoes that are perfect for salads, then make sure to consider Black Cherry, Elfin, and Gold Nugget Cherry. If you are looking for a slicer tomato, then make sure to consider Beaverlodge, Bush Beefsteak and Early Wonder. Careful examine the package, because you will discover tomatoes by the same name that are F1 and will not reproduce the same fruit the next season.

Varieties: If you are looking to grow cherry tomatoes indoors, then consider Patio, Micro Tom and Scarlet Pixie. If you love larger tomatoes, then make sure to consider Tiny Tim, Mountain Spring, Celebrity and Sungold.

Containers: For smaller tomatoes, especially bush varieties, containers that are at least 12 inches in depth are perfect. If you are interested in growing larger tomatoes, then consider growing each tomato in its own five-gallon bucket. The great news is that you can obtain these from many restaurants for free. Be sure to punch good drainage holes in the bottom.

Planting: Seeds should be planted 1/4 inch deep. By the seventh day, the seeds should have sprouted.

Temperature and Light Requirements: Tomatoes thrive at temperatures around 75 degrees. They require 14 hours of light each day. One problem that many gardeners encounter when raising tomatoes, especially bigger varieties, is splitting. If this is an issue for you, then chances are your grow lights are too close.

Watering Requirements: Your tomatoes need between an inch and two inches of water each day. While tomatoes require lots of water, make sure to not keep the water soggy, as it creates conditions for tomato diseases. Watch your tomatoes in the morning; if they are disease free and look wilted, then chances are you need to water.

Harvesting: The length of time to maturity varies widely. Therefore, you need to check on your individual variety. Cherry tomatoes can mature in as few as 45 days, while larger tomatoes can take twice that long.

Seed Saving: In order to save tomato seeds, make sure that it is an open-pollinated variety. Then, cut the tomato in half from top to bottom. Now, squeeze the gel and seeds into a container. Add 1/4 cup water and set in the sun for four days. A film will form which may look moldy. On the fourth day, remove the film and add more water. Stir gently and watch for the seeds to sink. Pour the water off. Then, add new water. Pour it off gently. Continue until no more pulp comes out with the water. Gather the seeds and let them dry on a paper plate. Once they are dry, store them in an airtight container.

Peppers

There are many different types of peppers that can be easily grown in an indoor garden. Growing a variety allows you to choose the ones that you like best. Almost all varieties are high in Vitamin C.

Heirloom Varieties: There are literally thousands of different varieties of peppers. Open-pollinated jalapeno peppers and banana peppers are a great choice and grow very easily. Habanero peppers are another popular choice including Red, Mustard and Peach. The best heirloom hot peppers include Cascabella, African Devil, Big Jim, and Black Hungarian. Indoor gardeners looking for bell peppers also find many terrific choices including Bullnose, California Wonder and Charleston. Those who prefer sweet peppers need to explore Chervena Chusha, Golden Calwonder and Cayenne.

Varieties: Just like with heirloom varieties, there are thousands of choices that grow well in indoor containers. Some great choices when looking for a sweet pepper include Early Pimento, Bell Boys and Gypsy. If you prefer a hot pepper, then make sure to consider Anaheim, Cayenne Long, and Serrano. Of course, you can always raise jalapeno and banana peppers that are not open-pollinated.

Containers: You cannot choose a container that is too big for a pepper plant. These plants have massive root systems that need room to grow for the best results. If you expect the mature pepper plant to be under 12 inches tall, then use a two-gallon container. Alternatively, if you expect the mature plant to be larger, choose a 10-gallon container.

Planting: Before you stick your pepper seed in the ground, you should soak it for a minimum of six hours. While plain water will work, the best solution for soaking is a solution of 3 percent hydrogen peroxide to a cup of warm water. Then, plant the seeds 1/4 inch deep in its own container.

Temperature and Light Requirements: Peppers love the heat. Therefore, make sure that your temperatures are always above 75 degrees. Most peppers can tolerate temperatures up to 87 degrees. Many people report having the best luck growing these tropical plants by continuously using heat pads on the bottom of the pots as well as growing lights. Peppers need at least 14 hours of light each day.

Watering Requirements: Peppers grown indoors require a lot more water than those grown in the outdoor garden. The best way to see if your plant needs watering is to stick your finger about four inches down into the pot. At that level, the soil should feel moist. If it does not, then it is time to water. If you like heat in your peppers, then water less frequently as the fruit ripens.

Harvesting: Most sweet peppers will be ready for harvest about 90 days after you plant the seed. Other varieties take much longer up to 175 days. If you want to increase your harvest, then harvest as soon as possible. If you leave green peppers on the plant longer, they may turn various colors. When you are harvesting sweet peppers, make sure to wear gloves and use pruners, as the oil from the pepper may hurt your skin.

Seed Saving: Harvesting pepper seeds from open-pollinated fruit is easy. Simply cut the fruit open and collect the seeds onto a paper plate ensuring they are in a single layer. Then, allow the seeds to dry until they are firm and are no longer flexible. Be sure to allow them to dry in an area that is under 90 degrees. Once the seeds are dry, store them in an airtight container.

Eggplants

Eggplants are grown around the world, and some of the best eggplants to grow come from foreign destinations. The humble eggplant can be prepared in so many different ways, so make sure to plant plenty.

Heirloom Varieties: Indoor gardeners can find a large supply of open-pollinated heirloom seed available on the market. You may want to consider growing Cambodian Green Giant, Diamond, and Rosa Bianca.

Varieties: If you want an oval eggplant, then consider Black Beauty, Dusky and Black Magic. Alternatively, if you prefer an elongated eggplant, then consider Ichiban, Little Fingers and Slim Jim. While most eggplants found in supermarkets are deep purple in color, gardeners have the choice of growing white eggplants. Some of the best varieties include Casper and Easter Egg.

Containers: Eggplants need to be grown in containers that are at least two gallons in size.

Planting: Eggplants need great drainage so start out by putting an inch of small size gravel in the bottom of the pot and then fill with your normal soil mixture. Seeds should be planted 1/4 inch deep. Eggplants need support so you will either need to place a bamboo stake in the middle of the cage or use a tomato cage. As plants mature, connect the plant to the stake or cage using plastic twine.

Temperature and Light Requirements: Eggplants like temperatures about 75 degrees, but will tolerate temperatures as low as 70 degrees and as high as 85 degrees. They need lights about 13 hours each day.

Watering: Eggplants like wet, but not soggy, soil. Therefore, it is important to water them on a regular basis. The best way to water an eggplant is to give it a good soaking in a tub of water.

Harvesting: It is vital to harvest an eggplant at just the right time to avoid a bitter taste. Watch your fruit carefully and notice when it stops growing larger. At this point, it should have lost its glossy shine to its skin. It is impossible to pick them by hand, so you will need to use sheers. Cut a small piece of the stem off with the eggplant.

Seed Saving: Gardeners find it easy to save seeds from an eggplant. Start by letting the plant become overripe on the plant ensuring that it does not touch the soil. At this point, it will turn translucent and shriveled. Then, cut the eggplant open and scoop out the seeds and the pulp. Put the seeds and pulp in some water. The good seeds will sink to the bottom of the bowl. Carefully pour the pulp, water, and bad seeds off. Repeat this process until no more pulp comes off in the water. Now, pour the seeds into a colander to remove as much water as possible. Lay the seeds on a glass plate and allow them to dry completely. This normally takes about a week. Store the seeds in an airtight container.

Radishes

There are numerous varieties of radishes available to indoor gardeners. Radishes are so easy to grow. If you have children who want to help you garden, they make a great first crop.

Heirloom Varieties - There are many wonderful varieties of heirloom radishes. Some of the best include Early Scarlet Short Top, White Turnip, and Yellow Summer. After all, not all radishes have to be round and red.

Varieties - Some of the best varieties of radishes include Cherry Belle, White Icicle and Dukon. When choosing a variety make sure to consider how long it takes the radish to grow to maturity because there is more variation in radishes than in almost any other vegetable.

Containers - The type of container that you will need to grow your radishes differs depending on the type of radish that you are growing. If you are growing long radishes, then you need a container that is at least 12 inches deep. Short and round radishes only require a container that is six inches deep. All containers should have a diameter of at least 12 inches.

Planting Radish seeds should be soaked for six hours before they are planted to soften the hard outer shell. Then, plant them 1/4 inch deep.

Temperature and Light Requirements - Radishes are a cool weather crop. They thrive best when temperatures are kept about 63 degrees. They also prefer light only about six hours a day. In fact, most radishes can thrive in south-facing windows without any grow lights at all.

Watering Requirements Radishes need consistent watering, but do not like soggy soil. Let the soil dry out slightly between watering.

Harvesting Make sure to watch your radish tops carefully for signs that it is time to harvest. You should begin pulling one or two a day until they get the size that you desire. Leaving radishes too long will result in hollow radishes that are starchy and do not taste good.

Seed Saving In order to save radish seeds, you need to let the radish grow a seed head in the soil. After the seed head has developed, pods will grow on the seed head. Let the plant continue to grow and the seed pods will dry out. After the seed pods dry out, you can simply save them this way until you are ready to plant. When you are ready to plant, remove the seeds from the pod and plant.

Potatoes

Potatoes can easily be grown indoors. That way, you can have fresh potatoes all year around. This plant is fascinating to watch in its different stages of development.

Heirloom Varieties - While heirloom varieties are great, most produce, that is often not the case with potatoes. Older varieties are just not as disease resistant as the newer varieties of potatoes. If you would like to grow heirloom potatoes, then try Bliss Triumph, Champion and Early Ohio.

Varieties There are many great varieties of potatoes that can be grown. Carefully consider the type of potato that is right for you. Russet potatoes are perfect for frying, baking and mashing. If you want to grow Russet potatoes, then consider Canela, Norkotah, and Rio Grande. Red potatoes are perfect for mashing and are used in many salads. If you want to try growing red potatoes, then consider Cherry Red, Colorado Rose and Mountain Rose. Alternatively, if you want to grow white potatoes that are perfect for roasting or steaming, then consider Foremost and Rocket.

Containers You can use almost any type of large container to grow potatoes. In fact, ingenious people have even built wooden boxes where potatoes can be planted on top of earlier planted potatoes. The idea here is that you can remove the bottom board, and harvest those potatoes while allowing the upper potatoes to continue to grow. This may save you a lot of room if you plan on growing many potatoes. At a minimum, you need a container that is at least 12 inches deep and 18 inches across.

The easiest way to grow potatoes is to sprout them in a glass of water. Cut the potato around the eye with a knife dipped in rubbing alcohol. Place the potato in a glass of water using toothpicks to hold it in place. The bottom third of the potato should be in the water. Once the potato has at least one stem, transplant it into soil.

Temperature and Light Control Potatoes need at least six hours of light each day. Potatoes are a cold weather crop that does best when soil temperatures are about 45 degrees.

Watering Requirements Potatoes can require up to two inches of water a day. Concentrate on watering at the base of the potato where the stems emerge from the ground.

Harvesting Potatoes are ready to harvest when tubers can be seen on the part of the potato that is above the ground. Small potatoes, however, can be dug a little ahead of that while other potatoes are left in the ground to mature.

Seed Saving If you let the potato continue to grow, it will eventually produce tubers. These tubers will produce berries that can be harvested and planted.

Conclusion

Thank you again for downloading this book!

I hope this book was able to help you to learn to grow an indoor garden.

The next step upon successful completion of this book is to actually design and grow your very own indoor garden.

Thank you and good luck with your own indoor garden!

Review

Thanks again for purchasing and reading *this book*.

As a self-published author, I love to know what the reader thinks. ☺ If you have a moment, please leave a review for my book on Amazon. It would be greatly appreciated. You can also check out all of my other books on my Amazon Author Central page.

Thank you!

Made in the USA
San Bernardino, CA
03 January 2016